The Boyfriend Bible

A man's translation of the woman's expectation of men

By
Jason T. Strohbehn

ISBN

978-0-578-00776-2

Dedication

I would like to dedicate this book to my beautiful Jennifer. Thank you for teaching me about of the top-secret world of women. Your patience, love, and understanding have given me a whole new life.

You have been my educator, my inspiration, my proofreader, my editor, my true love, my friend, my harshest critic, and my biggest fan. You really are my muse.

And for every time I have ever failed to live up to the ideal in this book, I am sorry. I love you and can't imagine my life without you. I will keep trying because you are worth it.

Appreciation

I would like to thank my friends and family for their love and support while I played author.

To Dad: I love you. Our road has not always been the smoothest but I have learned a lot from you over the years in both the do and don't category. You were right far more often than you were wrong. Read my book just in case this is one of the times when I'm right.

To Shannon: No matter where we are today, I will always value what we had. You are a great friend and an amazing mother for our kids. Thank you for traveling the hard roads with me while I tried to grow up. Make your next relationship the one you deserve.

To my son Tyler: Read this now. It will save you from getting your ass beat by girls for the rest of your life. I love you buddy.

To my daughter Riana: Make every man you date read this book. If they can't meet this standard, they are not good enough for you. I love you little princess.

To my publisher, Story Publishing of Cheyenne, WY: Thanks for having the faith to put your name on my great literary masterpiece.

To Jane and Shareen at Bouquets Unlimited in Cheyenne, WY. It's cool having family in the flower business. Love you both.

Finally, I would like to thank that elusive top-secret organization that all women seem to belong to for not killing me for so many years of bad behavior. I hope this pays my tab.

Contents

The Boyfriend Bible... i
Dedication iii
Appreciation... iv
Contents vi
Prologue 1
Don't Be a Wuss 4
Women in the Wild.. 6
Don't Treat Them Like You Want to Be Treated........ 18
It Was Funnier In Your Head....................................... 26
Chivalry Is Not Dead and Other Little Things............. 34
How to Raise Your Score.. 41
Surviving Insanity 53
Romantic Ideas... 60
That Was Dumb 81
Conclusion 95

Prologue

I was with the same woman for sixteen years before we finally woke up one day and realized that somewhere along the line our relationship had gone from love to friendship. It was on that morning, Shannon looked at me and said, "I don't want to do this anymore". I agreed. $500 dollars later, we were divorced, our child custody issues were settled, and I was looking for a place to live. My ex and me are still best friends, but we seem to lack that odd little spark that makes a marriage work.

When we broke up, I started dating and I found that women are crazy. There seemed to be a double top-secret organization of women which I began to call, "The Sisterhood" which regulated every aspect of a woman's existence. There seemed to be so many unwritten rules and nuances that I didn't have a prayer of figuring it out. I did try, but despite my best little efforts, I could never quite get it right. So… I ran back to my ex.

Oddly enough, the second time around, it only took us two years to realize that people are exes for a reason and that she and I were really better off apart. I was going to have to learn to make it on my own. To succeed, I was going to have to crack the secrets of The Sisterhood. I'm kind of a chunky kid with short hair and a deep voice so trying to go undercover in this organization was really out of the question. All of the women I am friends with would give me "the look" when I tried to question them on the topic. I think they were secretly trying to protect me.

Finally, after much searching, I found a woman who was not only a card-carrying member of The Sisterhood but also fell in love with me. I finally had my angle to learn what it was that I needed to keep a relationship alive with an amazing woman. Once I started to learn the secrets, I figured that men everywhere should probably be advised of the potential to have a happy relationship with a woman. I also learned that I could understand my woman better than

70% of the time without the aid of a translator or heavy medications.

Men… if you want to be able to keep a relationship alive and strong, follow the methods in this book to improve your communication and develop an understanding of the women in your life. With this book, you will be able to avoid some of the common pitfalls in relationships and to understand exactly what the hell the woman in your life is talking about when she wakes up mad because you were acting like an ass in her latest dream.

Don't Be a Wuss

Often times men choose not to make good relationship decisions because of the inevitable comments that they will get from some of their (probably single) friends. Men are worried about being accused of being pussy whipped or being told that their testicles are in a box on their girlfriend's nightstand. As funny as this may sound, most men respond to the pressure of such comments.

In the very short term, the guy response of saying, "screw it" and going with his friends has a payoff. The man gets to immediately go out and play and have fun. The man might even make a little profit if there are sports or gambling involved and will probably come home in a really good mood.

In the mid to long term, the approach of massaging the relationship with the woman has a significant payout that is often overlooked by the man in the throws of being called a wuss. First, the man doesn't have to come home to a pissed off woman and fight about his behavior and kill a perfectly good buzz. More importantly, the guy can build a strong relationship with his woman that will ultimately allow him to go out with his friends on occasion without fear of the fight afterwards. This can only be done by a man who is willing to put his girl first and spend time showing her that she is the most important person in his life. Once the relationship is stable and the trust is in place, the man can then arrange his days with the boys and still have plenty of time to be with his girl. It truly is a win-win scenario.

As a man, the long-term win would be to have the best of both worlds. Having a girlfriend that can be part of your life on a day-to-day basis, can be friends with your friends, and ultimately allows you some autonomy is the ideal. To pull this off, you first need to work on having a different kind of relationship with your girl. You have to understand her and work to meet her needs as well as your own.

Women in the Wild

This is the point where I feel like Steve Irwin should be jumping out from behind a rock yelling "Crikey, look at that one ovah there."

Women are remarkable, and I have found some things that they seem to have in common. First and foremost, most women come from a common set of social constructs. From the very beginning of man's relationships with women, men have been the hunter/gatherer and women have been the nurturer and caretaker. When we lived in caves, teepees, tents, and maybe even log cabins; this was a successful model. However, in today's society, it takes two wage earners to make ends meet and often times women are given the right message but don't see the follow through. Women are generally told to be equal and independent but what they see is a society where men have more opportunities than they do. We, as a society, are just now getting away from dumbing girls down in math and science and recognizing that although we may be wired a little different, women are equal to men in intellect as well as social skills and earning power.

Another thing that women have in common is that, in American culture, it is more acceptable for a woman to show emotions in public or group forums than men. As a result, women are often more free to wear their heart on their sleeve and more in touch with the emotions that drive some of their behaviors. This creates the first gap that men and women have to overcome when they try to unite as a couple because men have been taught to repress and that big boys don't cry... unless they accidentally break their favorite beer mug or throw a Wii remote through the 48" flatscreen LCD they just bought.

Women often do not have the pure physical mass that men possess. Men have been raised from little boys to honor the hunter/gatherer tradition by learning to fight and valuing those with bigger muscles and more testosterone. In short, men can be emotionally more distant, physically more powerful and have a sense of social entitlement that can create a third factor that many women share. Unfortunately many women have been the victims of a man's behaviors. Victimization isn't always physical or verbal abuse, sometimes it is simply that the man "turns off" and cannot acknowledge or meet the woman's social and emotional needs. This means that the man who is reading this book may already be behind the eight ball because her jackass ex-boyfriend didn't read this book.

Finally, another similarity that women seem to share is that they are generally more social than men. Men need to realize that this works in their favor because it keeps the women trying to like them, even when they are far short of ideal. Women are more comfortable doing things in packs than men will ever be. A group of three women can comfortably head to the bathroom together. Unless men are leaving an airplane or theater, they tend to carefully time their liquid consumption to allow them to avoid everyone they know in the bathroom. Women tend to like parties where the guests can talk and interact. Men prefer parties where interaction is limited to a high five when their team scores. Women appear less frequently in bars, restaurants, and other places alone; this can make them quite difficult to single out from the herd. It does, however, give men a good opportunity to watch them interact and to spot those subtle differences which make them so much fun.

For all of their similarities, there are some key differences between women that you need to be aware of if you are going to be successful in your relationships with them. For the purposes of this book, none of those differences relate to the size, shape, color, texture, taste or proportion of any body part.

In my field experience, I have identified five major subspecies of women: The Nester, The Runner, The Buddy, The Gold Digger, and Sorry Wrong Number. For those men who believe that I have omitted the ever-popular "Booty Call," I would argue that women always have an underlying type provides a more general guide to their behavior. This underlying type tells you why they are giving up the booty. Keep in mind that no woman is all one type, they have a little of each aspect in their personality, but with a little time, you should be able to identify the dominant trait.

The Nester

Men, if you want to find a woman who will have your dinner on the table when you get home and let you be the "Man of the House" this girl is for you.

The Nester is a woman who has bought fully into the idea that men are the provider and that women are the caretakers. If she likes you, this is the woman who tells you she is falling in love with you on the first date and has picked out your wedding cake by the third. The nester is most happy when she is in a relationship; especially in one where she feels valued and loved.

The Nester can be identified because they often have very few close friends. Those friends that they do have are rarely mentioned after you start dating them because you become the center of their world. The Nester may seem weak, but don't let appearances fool you. Once she has her ideas on life laid out, The Nester can be tenacious and difficult. At the extreme end, men will describe this type of girl with a story that starts out like this: "Dude, you ain't gonna believe what that crazy bitch did...."

On the positive side, Nesters will put up with more of a man's behaviors than most other types. A Nester will typically not really care how you dress or what you do as long as you come home occasionally and provide some tie to the "Leave it to Beaver" lifestyle that they crave. Nesters will normally abandon their close associations in favor of a man and may be willing to change everything about their life in order to make themselves more appealing to their man. For a man who wants to be in charge and have a woman who will probably be faithful with little or no effort, this is the way to go.

A word of caution… Nesters are not all sugar and spice. When scorned, the Nester can become a frightening sight that you will probably see parked outside of your work, your house at 2am, your new girlfriends house, your favorite bar and the gym where you started taking kickboxing to defend yourself from her crazy ass. In fact, all men should be required to watch a "Snapped" marathon on the Oxygen channel before dating a Nester. If you don't have cable, I would suggest renting "Fatal Attraction".

The Runner

Somewhere… Somehow… the Runner has been hurt. She isn't sure she really needs you around, but once you earn her love she's yours forever.

The Runner is a difficult bitch. She is stubborn and independent. She probably has a good job, her own life, her own friends, and her own ideas. If you are a weak man, the time to retreat is now because this woman will chew you up and spit you out if you are not willing to be a good boyfriend while hanging on to your own identity. The runner will probably have one or more close friends that she would never give up. These friends are the kind of people that would help heal your relationship or help her hide your body just depending on what was happening.

The runner is like the wolf in the movie "Dances with Wolves." She starts out slow and only comes to you at her pace. Often she will run away just to see what you do. If you have enough patience and willingness to compromise, the runner will eventually keep coming back. Every time she does, her hurts will heal a little more and she will stay with you a little longer. Once you get into her heart, she will stay and be faithful as long as you are.

On the upside, the runner is generally independent, social, and smart. She will often have very specific ideas on what a relationship looks like but is willing to accommodate your ideas too. This is the girl who is with you because she wants to be. She won't be crazy unless you make her that way.

A word of caution… This girl can be like chasing the wind. Any man in her life had better be prepared for some ups and downs. If you chase her too fast, she will run and not come back. If you chase her too slow, she will get away. This woman is a delicate balancing act. Remember that she is with you because she wants to be not because she needs you. If you do her wrong, you probably won't be stalked; but I would still recommend watching a couple episodes of "Snapped."

The Buddy

If you fall for her, this woman will wreck your life and you will love her anyway.

When a man has a female buddy, the boundaries often get clouded. Men will engage in the social aspects of a relationship with this woman. They may go to the bar, watch sports, work, or just "hang" but the man is generally off the hook for any of the boyfriend duties. While it is truly cool to hang with a girl buddy while the boundaries are solid, this relationship carries with it some significant pitfalls if you are hoping for a relationship.

First and foremost, she doesn't approve of anyone you date. You will not approve of anyone she dates. Quite simply this is a function of time and access. If you or she is dating, you don't have the same amount of time together. If you do preserve your relationship, you will be facing a constant inquiry from your significant other as to the extent of your relationship with the The Buddy. Neither you nor she will acknowledge or understand this dynamic, but it will be there.

Also, The Buddy will always run around the back of they guy's mind as the "potential girlfriend." No matter what she looks like or the relationship status, this girl has infiltrated the guys group of friends and is one of the gang. Today, she is probably the only exception to everything you ever thought about women.

Word of caution… today as your buddy, she is one of the boys. If you want her to be your girlfriend, you will both have to realign your thinking. You can't marry one of the boys and expect to have a passionate loving relationship. She isn't going to want that either. If you and the buddy become more than buddies, she will expect you to start acting like her boyfriend. If you are not a good boyfriend then you face an ex who is in tight with all of your friends, knows your dirty secrets and probably has your signature and PIN number down pat. Before you travel this road with this girl, you'd better be sure.

The Gold Digger
Have wallet will travel.

Men, if you are wealthy or just pretend to be, this woman is lurking around your wallet. Dating a Gold Digger is often nothing more than the purchase of arm candy. Affluence is the greatest aphrodisiac for this girl and she will truly be yours for as long as you can afford her. If you are wealthy and don't care about getting used, then this girl is for you. You don't have to be a particularly good boyfriend to hang on to a gold digger as long as the wallet is open.

At first glance, the Gold Digger may appear to be a Runner. She will come closer then step away always holding the man just close enough to let him orbit around her and keep him in the game. As a rule, the Gold Digger will have a very specific emotional boundary that can't be crossed no matter how much the man works for it. She will typically minimize her relationship to the man when talking to family and friends but then play the doting girlfriend when the man is taking her out to an expensive restaurant or buying gifts. The key difference between a Runner and a Gold Digger is that there is the runner either moves forward or backward in the relationship and this movement is not dependent on the financial state of either party. With the Gold Digger money moves her closer and poverty moves her back.

The Gold Digger is not entirely unattainable to the man who knows what he is doing, but attempting to chase a Gold Digger carries significant risks. First, getting and keeping her attention long enough to woo her is expensive. Second, the man has to be on his "A-Game" to show her that there is love outside of money and he better be able to maintain this game for a long time. Finally, there is always a risk that the reformed Gold Digger will go back to her old ways and leave her man for the next fat wallet walking by.

Word of Caution…

Money's tight

Times are hard…

Don't let her have

Your credit card

Sorry Wrong Number

For one reason or another this one is not accessible to you. She might already be in a relationship with a guy who has read this book. If so, she's probably happy. She might not be interested in you. Or she might not be interested in men. Essentially, your best chance would be to make this one your buddy but you are not going to have a relationship with her now and maybe not ever.

Within the subset of each of these categories, we could probably continue to break down the women into all sorts of different sub groups but for the purpose of a broad understanding this is all we need and will refer back to it as we go. The remainder of this book assumes you have gone on some type of man safari and found one of these women and that you would now like to keep her around. As with every species, there is the possibility that you will find a rabid one. I recommend immediate catch and release.

Don't Treat Them Like You Want to Be Treated

There are some basic differences between men and women and how they show love, affection and express emotion. Essentially, men can be emotionally fulfilled if you grunt at them and hand them a cold beer. Women, on the other hand require more.

Communication Basics

When men are talking, they will typically stand or sit shoulder to shoulder. In prehistoric times, it allowed them to interact while watching for saber-toothed tigers that might want to make them into lunch.

In modern world, it also works well because it allows men to watch TV, or stand at a bar without compromising the basic communication body position that has served us so well for so many eons.

Women tend to communicate differently, they tend to be more comfortable sitting face to face than men, and they appreciate and receive verbal feedback as well as feedback from eye contact and facial expressions. In prehistoric times, it allowed them to form that crucial bond with babies and other members of the little prehistoric clan. Additionally, women tend to be more comfortable with higher levels of non-sexual touch with people they trust.

When a woman is talking to the side of a man's head, while he is watching TV, they assume he is not listening despite the fact that he heard and absorbed every word she said. Men fail to realize that women may have a hard time deciphering the grunt which means, "I'm listening" from the grunt which means "a darn good field goal attempt". When a woman wants to communicate with a man, she often tries to force that eye contact and face to face situation which men interpret one of two ways: First, she's in my space. Second, she wants to sleep with me because she's in my space. Sometimes neither of these things is the case and she just wants you to communicate in a manner that she is used to and comfortable with. She wants to see expressions on your face and hear you respond verbally to her discussion. Non-sexual touch is even a good idea here.

If you want to truly open lines of communication with a woman, you need to start by turning your entire body towards the woman so that your shoulders are mostly square to the woman. Make eye contact (with their eyes) and try not to look at her boobs or everything with boobs that goes by on the left or right. Once you make eye contact break it on occasion to avoid looking like a creepy stalker guy who just stares at people. Women will notice the effort and generally be a little forgiving until you've had time to adjust.

Once you have adjusted your body to open the lines of communication, you then have to look like you are paying attention. Paying attention means nodding in the right places, asking questions, and showing appropriate facial expressions and emotion. While men understand that the grunt has many varied meanings, which depend on the volume, duration, tone and intensity of the grunt; women don't get it. As a result, men should resort to actual voice communication with the use of full sentences and asking questions when talking to women.

An additional benefit of this type of communication is that it allows the man and woman to have intense eye contact that definitely increases the intensity of the relationship but also can serve as a tool to enhance the sexual attraction between the couple.

Word of Caution… If you are going to check out her cleavage from this position, you have to make sure you don't get caught. Looking down her shirt while she is trying to look into your eyes will get you busted. Instead, wait until she glances away then catch a quick glimpse down her shirt. This can often be done when she looks up towards a waiter or passerby or when she looks down to stir her drink in a club.

If you are caught, skip directly to the chapter on recovering from a screw up.

She's Not a Man

In case you missed the title, this book is about men learning the secrets of women. You cannot treat women the same way as you can treat a man and expect a favorable result. If you read nothing else in this book, read this section.

Men can see each other after a year apart and pick up right where they left off by saying, "Hey fuckwad get your chunky ass over here." Do not; ever, say this to a woman. Really. It is bad… don't do it. Women don't like to be cursed at, they do not like to be insulted and for the most part do not have even the slightest understanding of how men can find this type of interaction okay and funny. If you convert from Buddy to girlfriend, you can no longer throw this phrase at her and expect it to be okay. Yelling from the living room couch, "Hey bitch, bring me a beer" could go from funny to fatal based on the definition of relationship between the Buddy and her new beau.

When fighting with your woman, don't curse her and call her names or threaten her with physical violence. Men can throw the phrase, "Fuck you, I'm gonna beat your punk ass" at another man with little or no emotional problem. If you say things like this to a woman, you are not going to win your fight. You will make the situation worse and probably do emotional damage that you won't even understand until she bursts into tears three weeks later at your sister's wedding.

When arguing with a woman, avoid attacking her physical features, intellect, or self-esteem. Men find this an acceptable way of fighting with one another. If you are important to the woman, however, it just beats her down and doesn't solve the issue that caused the argument in the first place. A woman who is defeated and beaten is not able to be a functioning part of a relationship that will last. Ultimately she will leave you for someone who is not threatening or insulting.

Men get angry with other men and can demonstrate their overabundance of "pissedoffitude" by tipping over a table or throwing a chair. When surrounded by a bunch of similarly testosterone-laden individuals, this may be perfectly appropriate and even become the story that later legends are born from. When you are with your girlfriend, you need to realize that she probably won't be impressed by your ability to lift and throw a table unless she is underneath it and the building is on fire. In fact, most women would define this behavior as being an asshole. It is okay for you to be mad and have strong opinions but when you demonstrate that you have a complete inability to control your emotional state, women are not impressed.

Sometimes the only way to resolve an argument with another man is to have a good old-fashioned knock down, drag out fight. Very few things bring two men together like sobering up in a jail cell while trying to remember who broke whose nose first. This is not true of women. (Women are typically not raised to physically fight, especially with a man.) If you want a lasting relationship with a woman, then hitting her will not get you there. Assault on a woman is illegal and really just a pretty stupid way of demonstrating an inability to control and express anger and powerlessness. In looking at the basic characteristics established earlier in the book, we can see that women will generally have less body mass and raw physical strength than men. This should go back to a man's schoolyard lessons where he learned not to pick on someone smaller than he is and to stick up for the underdog.

Point to Remember… Big boys don't hit girls.

Ignoring an Issue Won't Make it Go Away

The "big boys don't cry" attitude that we are all raised with has taught us that repressing feelings and ignoring the problem can sometimes make it go away. If two men have a problem with each other and enough time passes, they will both be able to comfortably pretend the problem no longer exists. This does not work with a woman. If a woman believes that a problem exists and she ignores it, the problem will get worse. If the man ignores her attempts to resolve the problem, it will get worse. Essentially men and women have to communicate and resolve issues between them because otherwise the problems will get worse.

When a man and woman have a fight that is not fully resolved, the man should expect one of two results. Either you will talk about it again now or next time you fight, she will bring it up again. Get used to it. Women communicate verbally to resolve issues. As a man, you may see this as nagging but women typically start out communicating and only resort to nagging when you refuse to listen and engage.

Caution… Ignoring your issues will certainly make them go away. This will happen when the woman leaves.

It Was Funnier In Your Head

Ahhhhh the fine art of practical jokes, stupid jokes, childish jokes, and generally juvenile behavior. In the right crowd, these can really be an art form all their own. When used to flavor your day-to-day relationship these items can make your spouse feel like she's living in a frat house. Don't get me wrong; women love a good sense of humor. They even love some good old-fashioned adolescent antics. However, there are certain types of this behavior that are better appreciated than others.

To begin, lets look at some scenarios:

The Easy Scenario...

It is a cool dark night. You and your girl have turned in early for bed. It is clear from her body language that you probably ain't getting any booty, but she still wants to be near you. As she cuddles up next to you, the two-pound triple-decker burrito that you had for lunch is now screaming for just a little relief. The beans, rice, and eye-watering hot sauce have now formed a toxic brew that is inflating your colon like a balloon animal. In your mind, you know sex is out. You know that farts don't really stink if they are your own. You have a defenseless victim lying peacefully with her head against your chest.

Every man reading this saw the set up coming because, in your head, letting rip with an earthshaking fart and jerking the covers over her head while pinning her against your chest with a free arm is the funniest thing you can come up with. In her mind, this would be less than funny. In fact the cuddling and no booty probably indicates that she just wants to be reassured that you are in her life. Instead of the obvious low road, it is probably best to excuse yourself and run to the bathroom.

The Medium Scenario...

You have just gotten married. At your reception, you have the opportunity to grab the microphone and thank those in attendance. You make it through, thanking the father of the bride and all in attendance. You glance over at your buddies who are waiting expectantly for you to do something that redefines bad adolescent behavior. After drinking a lot of beer, you are a little bloated and feel like you might finally be able to get out the entire alphabet in one colossal burp.

The man answer here is to go for it. You have been on your best behavior all day. You showered, put on a tux, and even refrained from slapping the maid of honor on the ass when she stopped to cover the Motley Crue tramp stamp which was creeping out from the edge of her backless gown. Now just seems like time to throw out some juvenile behavior. Before you raise the microphone to your lips, however, you must realize that this should be one of the most exciting, romantic, and memorable days of your woman's life and it would not be well thought out to go for the record at this place and time. Women want their wedding to be more magical than a unicorn in a top hat pulling a rabbit from a monkey's butt. If you were in a pub or at home, she may be supportive of such a record setting feat, but the audience is not right for this performance.

The Hard Scenario…

It is her 40th birthday, you know she is a little traumatized so you and several of your closest buddies sneak home to get a party ready for her. Wanting to make her night special, you and your friends drink all the liquor in the house but thoughtfully go out and buy two kegs and blow up the 2500 black balloons that will fill the entire living room. In the middle of the black balloons she will not only find all of her party guests but also the thoughtful gift you got her… a new transmission housing for your Chevy.

As tough as it is, try to follow on this one. When a woman is traumatized, she may not want get rip roaring drunk surrounded by black balloons. If, however, this does not send your party down in flames, the gift needs to be carefully reworked before you place it oh so gently upon the gift table. Here I will introduce a critical concept. It would be a rare circumstance and woman who would find auto parts to be the perfect gift. Before her birthday, get to know her and think carefully about other things you've seen her buy. If she has never actually used the phrase, "buy me auto parts for my birthday," I would suggest something more conventional like jewelry, clothing, or even some type of appliance. Auto parts, even high quality, expensive, and hard to find auto parts are not made for birthdays.

Cartoon Fun

Another common funny that men tend to over-appreciate is the cartoon. Occasionally or when the kids are around, it is okay to have a little Spongebob appreciation moment. When she is asleep on the couch, you could probably even throw a little Family Guy into the mix. However, as a general rule, you should oh so slightly reduce your cartoon consumption when you are with your girl. In the void that is now your cartoonless existence, you could try talking to your girl or even finding something to do together. One point, for God sakes… do not expect all but the rarest of women to truly appreciate the comic book collection that takes up a full room in your house, your action figure collection, or your cartoon character underwear. When you find a woman you want to keep, you may have to give up some of the artifacts of your childhood. As hard as this is to fathom, you may have to make some changes if you don't want to spend the rest of your life eating Cheetos and watching porn in your parent's basement. If you are not sure about the relationship, a storage facility is always a possibility until you grow up a notch or two.

Joke Telling

Certain categories of jokes are less likely to be appreciated by women. Examples include: Body functions, prostitutes, anybody with the same hair color as your girl, dead things including cats, and poor woman drivers. Not all jokes are off limits, the trick here is to know your audience. If you girlfriend is a blond prostitute going to mortician school she may find some of these jokes funny. Similar rules apply to stories. Men can listen to other men talk shit all day long. The only thing for men that is more fun than hunting and gathering is lying about how well they hunted and gathered. Women... not so much. When every story ends with a punch in the eye or a fart, women tend to get tired of hearing them. Think of story telling to your girl as a variety act. You can talk about your work, but also talk about hers. Discuss issues that matter to her. If you were going to tell a story that ends with a good fart punchline, I would involve alcohol early in the process.

Joke timing is another key thing that should not be underestimated here. When your girl has just wrecked her car, it is not a good time to tell bad driving jokes. When she gets really really drunk and barfs in her car, it is a bad time to start referring to the car as the vomit comet or the barfmobile. Don't refer to her as Barferella or the Princess of Puke. All of these things could be funny later or if she were a guy. Neither condition exists so drag yourself into boyfriend mode, hold her hair back, and try to see the football game from the bathroom. If your girlfriend does barf, you will have to help clean it up. Get over it. If she were a guy, you would carefully select jokes here about needing a spoon or straw for the cleanup. Your girl won't think this is funny.

Practical Jokes
Practical jokes can be a fun and creative way to express your feelings or to enjoy a good laugh. It is wise, however, to think about the end result of the joke before it happens. For example, it is not wise to creep into the bedroom and scare your girl in a Halloween mask if you bought her a shotgun for self-defense the week before. Any joke that causes your girl to clean up body fluids (hers or others) should probably be avoided at all costs. Yes, gentlemen, this includes the classic plastic wrap on the toilet gig. A practical joke that

involves sending fake officers to her work to strip should be carefully thought through. This is especially true if any of the officers are over 400 lbs. Finally; any practical joke that involves your penis in a fake gift box is only good for one laugh. After that it's just creepy. For clarification, pizza boxes and shoeboxes are included in the one time rule.

Chivalry Is Not Dead
and Other Little Things

First and foremost, women are smart, independent and do not need us. As a man you ride up to the tower on your white horse to save her only to find that the damsel isn't really in distress. She made a rope from her bed sheets, climbed down from the tower and is now in the woods killing the dragon to make a really cool purse. That said… most women enjoy a little spoiling and gentlemanly behavior. If you are a man who is trying to grow or keep a relationship, it will live or die on the little things. If you are a man with a crappy job who is trying to catch a beautiful woman who is way out of your league, this is your only prayer.

Chivalry

Chivalry in the modern world has gotten tougher. As a man, you know it is hard to know when to hold the door, pull out a woman's chair, pay a compliment or defend her honor. When you are in your day-to-day life, outside of a relationship, the answer is particularly gray. When, however, you are in a relationship, the answer is a little clearer. Chivalrous behavior in a relationship is always appropriate as long as you don't get too creepy with it. For example, pulling out her chair in a fast food restaurant may be a little much, but in a nice restaurant; it should be the rule rather than the exception.

Never underestimate the power of holding a car door for your woman. It takes no time or effort, but when she is trying to juggle her purse and all the crap you've handed her to carry she will appreciate some common courtesy. These little things show her you care.

The modern man knows that chivalry is as much about being a gentleman as it is about anything else. A man who remembers to say "please" and "thank you" and to be considerate of those around him will make a far better impression than those who constantly have the dial set to "rude." Chivalry is about how you treat people around you besides the woman in your life. Do you tip well when appropriate? Can you resolve problems with service or products without having a screaming fit? How do you treat your friends and family? All of these are questions that give a woman insight into how you will treat her.

Defending her honor is a tough road unless the man remembers that it doesn't always mean a confrontation or a fistfight. Sometimes it is as simple as gently reminding his friends and family of the woman's importance and of his intolerance for those that want to speak badly of her. Complimenting your woman to your friends, even when she's not around, can defend her honor without picking a fight. When it comes time to stand up for your woman physically, it is wise to know exactly what her stance on this would be. She may be fiercely independent and want to handle things herself to a point. In this case, you need to make sure she knows you are there to save her if things out of hand. In other cases, women would like to step back, let you strap on your shining armor, and ride to the rescue. You will only know what she prefers if you are communicating with her.

Day-to-Day Things

Everyday show your girlfriend that you love her. Take time to do the little things every day and the big things come much easier. Little things that a man can do every day that don't cost much money but will make your relationship stronger include:

- Tell her you are thinking of her. Just send a random text message to her that says... "Thinking of you."
- Pick something you like about her and tell her.
- Open the car door when you go somewhere, even if it is just the grocery store.
- Send an email.
- Try to get in her pants.
- Put her first... let her have the first shower or the first cup of coffee in the morning. Let her choose lunch or dinner plans. Let her know you care by asking for and respecting her opinion.
- Take charge... Once in a while when she seems receptive to it, just take charge. Whether it is something as simple as where you are going or what you are doing, sometimes taking charge can be a challenging and thrilling thing for her. Don't do it all of the time.

- Surprise her with a little note in her purse.
- Rub her feet.
- Rub her back.
- Lean over and kiss her or swat at her playfully when she walks by.
- Dance with her in the kitchen.
- Sing her a love song.

These are all simple ideas that take little time, little money, and will go a long way towards showing that you have a true interest in your girl. Once your relationship with her grows, you will learn which of these she really likes and how far you can take some of them. For example, you may be able to turn a foot rub into a night of unbridled passion... then everyone wins.

The Concept of Beauty

Every man wants to be with a beautiful woman. Each of us has a little different taste. Whether you like 'em skanky, classy, skinny, heavy, athletic, soft, blonde, brunette, bald, tall, short, old or young; there is someone out there for you. When you are looking for a woman to share your life, there are just a few rules to keep in mind when it comes to beauty. The first rule is that a man must know his limitations. Before you decide to go off in search of the perfect woman, you should probably look at yourself critically. You should look at what you have to offer in all areas of his life including appearance, job, social skills, and stability and decide what you can realistically find in a relationship. As a general rule, you need to realize that you are not going to find and keep a "10" if you are a "2".

The second rule of beauty for men is: Never settle. If you are going to have a relationship with a woman, she should be what you want. Think of getting into a relationship as buying a car. If you want a brand spanking new Dodge Challenger with the big engine, you wouldn't buy a 1993 Suzuki Esteem with the 1.6L engine and expect to be as happy. The same is true with women. If you can't look at your woman and see the most beautiful woman in the world, you should probably evaluate whether or not your desires are realistic and whether or not the relationship is going to get past your issues.

Once you are with a woman and you believe she is the most beautiful woman in the world, tell her. Tell her sincerely and honestly. After you tell her, then show her. You can show her how beautiful she is by taking her out around your friends and family. When you are with her, don't check out every other girl who walks past. When she is on your arm, smile and be proud. This is a good time for the little swats and playing that are mentioned above. Women enjoy feeling like they are beautiful and you appreciate them. Men will find that the more beautiful a woman feels, the less likely she is to stray and the more likely she is to be the fun, social and uninhibited woman you are going to enjoy most.

How to Raise Your Score

To be perfectly candid, it is important for men to realize that women are as like to score us on the famous "1-10" scale as we are likely to score them. Except for the extremely handsome, rich, or refined men, most of us are going to score about a six. Get used to it. Fortunately, unless you are just hideous, there are ways you can raise your score by a point or two without undergoing any major surgery.

Know the Game

Every victory in battle follows great intelligence gathering. It is important to realize that finding and maintaining a solid romantic relationship is no less complicated than storming the beach at Normandy. A solid use of intelligence gathering can help you turn certain defeat into a romance. Like military intelligence gathering, you are going to want to start at the global level and work down to the individual human level when you gather your intel. At the farthest macro level, you want to be aware of issues affecting women. If you want to be the true relationship guy, it wouldn't hurt to take a women's issues course at your local college. In lieu of this, there are simpler things you can try. I recommend picking up a magazine or two and studying. Giving a quick read to Cosmopolitan magazine is going to teach you things about women you are not sure you even wanted to know. You will learn not only what they feel and think, but you will gain valuable insight into the way they see men. Additionally, Cosmo has many sections each month that give things from a man's point of view. You need to know what counter intelligence has been done on men and what accurate and inaccurate information women have been given. Don't worry guys, its not all perfume and daisies. Cosmo has some of the greatest sex stories and pictures of women in lingerie that you've ever seen.

If you're feeling particularly brave you will look at other women's magazines as well. Learning what women are seeing about women's and men's fashion, relationships, careers, and social outlets all gives you an edge when the woman in your life is talking to you about the things which are important to her.

On an individual level, you should know some very specific things about your girl. First and foremost you need to realize that dates, times, and places have a higher level of significance for women than they do for men. Specifically, you should have a very good grasp of the following things:

- When and where you met.
    o Knowing some detail here always gives extra points.
- Know important dates for the relationship such as anniversaries. If you are dating a Nester, it might be good to know how long you've been together down to the 10th of a second.
- Know her birthday.
- Know, roughly, the important dates in her life.
- Does she have pets? What kind? What are their names?
- Does she have kids? Their ages? Their names? Their birthday?
- What are her parent's names? Where do they live?

- Favorite color?
- Clothing size?
- Jewelry preference and size?

This list could go on for the entire length of the book. Men need to realize, however, that more information gives them a better likelihood of being successful in the relationship.

Word of Caution – Gathering information through conversation and exchange of ideas and concepts is perfectly appropriate. Hiding in her bushes and rummaging her garbage is not.

Physical Appearance

Like you, your woman will have a picture of the ideal man in her head. You can safely assume that you are at least kind of close or else she would probably not be with you. Some of your intelligence gathering is well spent figuring out what the physical attributes of her perfect man are and working towards that end. Begin with the quick stuff... clothing.

If your girlfriend wears name brand clothing and makes an extra effort to be pretty around you, it is safe to assume that your "I'm with stupid" t-shirt, ripped blue jeans, and uncombed hair probably is not the look you should be striving for. Conversely, if your girl is dressing down and going without makeup or combed hair, it is safe to say that your khaki pants and golf shirts for a lazy day might be just a little bit much. For the sake of this book, I am assuming that men can figure out how to throw on jeans and a t-shirt for the dress down occasions, and I'm going to focus on dressing up.

If your girlfriend looks good and you want to look good for her, have her take you shopping. I know, this sounds horrifying and will involve time in a dressing room, but it is worth the pain. In having your girlfriend dress you up, you will have clothing that she thinks is nice and you will also get a good picture of what she does and doesn't like so later you can shop on your own. This also provides a good time to bond with the woman in your life and to show her that her opinion of you matters. As a man, you are expected to have some level of resistance here so occasionally argue (just a little) about going into the dressing room or hold up some particularly horrifying outfit for her to shoot down. The result will be that you will both have a fun time.

When shopping with a woman, you have two choices. First, you can drag your feet and mope. This will not end well. Your second choice is to simply have fun with it. This has the big benefit of giving your girl and you some great time to bond. If that isn't enough, you can relish in the fact that and it really pisses off all of the men in the store who are moping because they get to be yelled at all the way home by a woman who wants to know why they can't be more like you.

After dealing with the clothing, a man should consider his hair situation. First and foremost, find out what she likes. If you have any excessive hair problems such as eyebrows like a muppet, ear or nose hair which is long enough to braid or back hair like a great ape, you may wanna enlist the services of a professional. Yes, you may have to get something trimmed, sculpted, waxed or lasered but if it gets you more booty, it is well worth it. After you resolve the excess hair situation, you should consider your remaining hair. At a minimum, keep it clean and combed. If you were going to do anything radical before you see your girl next, it would be wise to mention it to her and give her some input. For example, going from waist length hair to bald would be a bad move to make without her input. Changing hair color, length, and style are decisions that should be carefully considered. Most men, quite honestly, do not possess the intellectual horsepower to make this decision properly on their own. Involve her and you will be glad you did.

After you have the new clothing and before you put them on, it is a good time to look at your personal hygiene. Start at the top and comb your hair into whatever style your hairdresser tried to give you. After that, just work your way down the body. Make sure you hit all of the important parts such as the teeth, ears, armpits, crotch, butt, and feet. The personal grooming routine is not just limited to making sure things don't stink. You also need to make sure your nails are neatly trimmed, including your toes. Your girlfriend does not want to feel like she is sleeping with a rabid wolverine.

With the quick stuff out of the way, it would be a good time to look at your physical condition. If your woman likes her men big and squishy and you happen to fit the bill; then you are probably not going to worry about this too much. If, however, your woman likes her man to look a little leaner and stronger for health or cosmetic reasons, it may be a good time to look at ways to get there from here. Watching your diet and exercise is the key to making your body look better. Working out does not have to be a solitary endeavor. Find something that you and your girl like to do and go do it together. Whether it is taking a walk or kickboxing; your relationship and your body will be better for it.

Learn an Uncommon Skill

Pre-requisite required - When a woman and a man are together, she expects him to bring a certain set of skills to the table. Those skills generally include light maintenance and yard work, lifting heavy things, killing crawly things, and anything involving the garage, tools, and car. If you can't pull of very basic things in these areas, I would strongly recommend you start buffing up these skills immediately.

In relationships, women's biggest complaint is often that the man continues in his hunter/gatherer archetype and fails to realize that some of the home duties are best borne by two people instead of one. To be successful in a relationship the man should possess and be willing to use some basic home skills that will make everybody's life easier. Examples include:

Learn to Cook

Historically a woman did the cooking unless it involved an outdoor grill or open cooking fire in the woods. This stereotype continued even after women became a vital part of the workforce. Most women don't want to come home and cook after a hard day at the office but in many relationships it is the norm. To make things great with your woman, learn to cook. Don't just learn to open a can and heat the contents, learn to walk into a kitchen, grab crap off of the shelf, and pull off a restaurant quality dinner. If you can do this with only what you find and with no notice, you can truly be the MacGyver of the kitchen.

If you can't cook but you want extra points in this category, tell your girl that you don't really know how to cook and ask her to take a class with you. This gives her an opportunity to teach you what she knows and help you learn the foods she likes to eat. In lieu of this, get the most basic Betty Crocker cookbook on the market and start by following the recipes verbatim.

Help with Cleaning

Like cooking, cleaning was mostly a woman's realm and continued to be even after women entered the workforce fulltime. A man who can do some basic cleaning can really keep things happier at home. In order to shift cleaning into the realm of a man's mindset, the man needs to look at cleaning as an opportunity to buy some good heavy duty cleaning tools by Black and Decker and other top toolmakers. Helping around the house doesn't necessarily mean that the man has to put his high power, industrial tools away. Learn to do some of the jobs around the house very well. Do those jobs quickly and consistently and enjoy the benefit of a more harmonious home.

If you are really feeling in the mood to generate harmony at home, you could always suggest a beer, pizza, and cleaning night at home. The more fun approach here will give you a chance to do something good for your relationship without sacrificing the staples of manliness (beer, pizza, and a hot girl).

Learn an Artistic Skill

A perfect way to express your love for a woman is to do something that nobody else can do for her. One example is to make her something beautiful. If you can draw, learn to sketch her face. If you can paint, paint her a picture. If you like clay, learn to sculpt. In short, learn to do something that can be occasionally used to show your love.

Note of Caution – An occasional picture or sculpture is good, filling a three bedroom house with little clay figures of your girlfriend is creepy.

Learn a Couples Skill

Take a class with your girlfriend. Learn massage, learn to dance, learn to cook, or just take something that lets you work together for fun. Taking time to learn something new with your significant other will give you an opportunity to grow together and to have something that is really just exclusively yours as a couple. Massage and dance are fun because they let you be close together and to develop a deeper physical bond. Dancing provides a great way for you and your girl to show off together in public as well. Taking cooking or art are things that will generally be a more private experience for the two of you, but will let you find common interests.

After you learn your couple's skills, don't just let them die. If you learned to dance, take her dancing. If you learned to cook, cook something together. If you learned to massage, feel her up. In short, the class lets you experiment and try new things together, but doing them later allows you to relive the positive memories and build new ones.

Surviving Insanity

As a man, you will encounter occasions during a relationship where you are just sure that the woman in your life has just lost her damn mind. Unless she lost her mind as a direct result of your actions, it is important for you to realize that the woman is often times looking for a specific response from you or needs you to provide some level of comfort, support or understanding to her. Sometimes she knows she's being crazy and just needs you to be okay for her. She would do the same for you.

Providing Emotional Support

When a woman comes to a man and starts ranting about men, work, people, relatives, or anything else that the man did not cause. The man's response should be to listen and reassure. Unless asked, don't solve the problem for her. Men normally communicate to get to the point and solve the problem. Often times a woman communicates to discuss a problem and get support. Odds are she already knows how to solve the issue at hand. Most of the time a woman who has had a bad day needs a strategy consultant much less than she needs a boyfriend. In the role as boyfriend, it is your job to listen. If she starts hitting topics that are sensitive to you because they hit too close to home, shut up and listen. The last thing a woman wants to do is have the man in her life get defensive and start fighting back when the issue at hand has nothing to do with him. If you find yourself getting too sensitive over the things she's saying, it may be a good time to look at areas where you can support her better before the ranting is about you.

When providing emotional support, it is okay to ask if there is anything you can do to help. If she says there is, then do it. If not, just commiserate with the situation and let her rant. Again, she has probably done the same for you.

Providing the Right Answer

Every man's worst nightmare is the question… "Honey, does this make my ass look big?" This question and many others are an example of needing to read a situation and give the right answer. When deciding the right answer, the man must first know if the woman is looking for honesty or reassurance. To get to this understanding, the man should evaluate whether or not his answer will end up with the woman saying or doing something which would make her feel stupid or degraded. For example, letting your woman go to a party in a dress that is four sizes too small is not nearly as smart as giving her a true answer before she leaves.

Remember that the truth can hurt so deliver your answer in a tactful and smart way. For example, when asked if an outfit looks okay. Do not say, "No it looks like shit." Instead offer another route with a little different tone. You could answer, "It looks okay, but do you know which outfit is absolutely amazing on you?" Often times this will get you through the tough questions that require the whole truth. By approaching the issue this way, she will know that you thought she looked awful in the first outfit, but doesn't feel like you find her repulsive. This is another answer where you would probably answer a man with an insult that is not appropriate for the woman you love.

Questions that require a much higher level of tact and ability are those that are solely to provide your woman with emotional support and reassurance. These sentences will often require you to make direct comparisons with others. Am I prettier than... Am I a better kisser than... What do you like about me more than your ex... It is wise to remember here that your very life may be at stake in your answer. If you cannot answer these questions honestly and without hurting your girlfriend's feelings, you probably need to look carefully at the quality of your relationship.

Yeah... She's Nuts

Every woman can be a little crazy. When it happens you just have to deal with it in a supportive way that doesn't judge her or make her feel like an absolute whack job. For example:

A man and woman wake up in the morning and the woman is a little quiet and not quite herself. Finally she looks at the man and says that she had a terrible dream the night before. She dreamed the man turned into an absolute ass right before leaving her for his ex.

To the man, this is beyond crazy. He knows he would never do or act as he is said to have done. The man has two choices. He can dismiss the dream and her feelings as crazy or he can be an emotional support for his girl. If he chooses to dismiss the dream, the woman will probably continue to dwell on it and think about it for some time. She will test his actions against her memory of the dream and worry at the slightest hint of trouble. The man has no idea she is still crazy and goes about his business and probably doesn't even see a storm coming until they are fighting about something inconsequential and the dream is brought back into play in the form of… "See you are acting just like my dream." The man will be confused and the woman is pissed. Not a great relationship enhancing moment.

In the same scenario, the man can take an alternate course by spending a few minutes to talk about the dream with his girl. Possibly, he can even offer an apology and reassurance that it was just a dream and that he would never do anything to hurt the woman he loves. The woman may still worry or be a little upset for a while but in the end, she will feel supported and cared for so the damage will not be done.

A word of Caution – Don't laugh or poke at a crazy woman. She may just haul off and kill you. If in doubt, watch Snapped on the Oxygen Channel.

Opportunities for Emotional Bonding

When your woman is having a little crazy moment and you are there, you have an opportunity to show her how much you care and how important she is to you. Some tips for success include:

- Remember that, unless you caused her craziness, that it is not about you.
- Listen to her and empathize.
- If you didn't break it, you may not be able to fix it.
- She wants your support and not necessarily to be rescued.
- Be truthful and tactful.
- Understand that she is not the master of repressing feelings that you are.
- A hug or holding a hand can sometimes go a long ways.
- She probably won't see the humor in her craziness right now. Joking may not be good.
- Offer to help.

A man who can handle the crazy moments with grace and emotional availability can use the crazy times as a springboard for a strong connection that will make a relationship last.

Romantic Ideas

Romantic does not have to mean expensive. Romantic means you thought of your girl and put that thought into action in a way that allowed you and her to connect. It really is simple. Obviously this is not a comprehensive list, but it will give you a start as to some basic romantic ideas.

Day to Day Romance

Flowers at Work –

Why do women like flowers at work? Simple, it makes the other women jealous and shows that her boyfriend cares more than theirs. This romantic idea takes very little effort and just a couple hundred dollars on the part of a man to make it memorable. For extra points, don't call the order in. Actually go to the flower shop and hand write the card or send another special little gift along.

Flowers at Home –

If a man has a house key, giving flowers to his girl can be an adventure in and of itself. Putting the flowers somewhere unexpected or having flowers waiting for her when she is getting home from a trip or a hard day at work is a spectacular way to show her she's on his mind.

A NOTE ON FLOWERS

Learn the meaning of flowers before you give them. Flower colors and types all have a specific meaning that your woman will know. Those black roses in a gold vase may look really cool in the Loaf & Jug window, but they don't exactly scream romance.

Give flowers when things are good. If you only give her roses when you screw up, it won't have the positive effect you hoped for when you give them as a genuine gift.

Get the best flowers you can. If you can afford the best florist in town, get that. Don't be a cheap ass. Flowers aren't that pricey and a professionally designed bouquet is really the better way to go. A florist will steer you away from the ugly stuff that looks cool to you and towards things that girls like.

No Love For the Flowers?

If she is not a flower fan, don't give up. You can always find her something else that you know she will appreciate such as shoes, clothing, or a spa treatment appointment. Whatever you get her, remember that you are always better off if you get her more personal gifts rather than something too common. Also remember that you should confine gift deliveries to her work to romantic and appropriate items. Jewelry, flowers, candy, cards, and other nice romantic gifts are good things to have delivered to her work. Crotchless leather panties are not.

Give her a Massage –

Normally, a man gives a massage by rubbing the shoulders for two seconds then trying to jam his hands down the girlfriend's pants. My romantic suggestion would be different than the norm. Invite your woman to get naked except for a towel, and give her a massage using good massage oil down, rub her entire body. Avoid the ever-popular boob and crotch grab. If it puts her to sleep you win because she knows you are willing to go all out for her. If she feels sexual you win because you have laid the groundwork to continue to more sensual activities.

Send her a Text –

Just for no reason at all, send your girlfriend a text message telling her that you're thinking of her and that she's beautiful.

Make Her a Dinner –

Some night have a romantic dinner for two planned where you cook the entire dinner and have it waiting when she gets home. Do it right. Go with candles, wine and romantic music.

Quiet Night at Home –

Turn off the TV and get out her favorite food and drinks. Go to a comfortable spot in the house and just hang out and talk. Sometimes the talk will be light and easy, but others will be deep and intense. This is an entire evening event, so don't bother trying to wedge it in between the five o'clock news, and a football game you want to watch.

Grab Her Hand –

Just for no reason at all, reach out and grab your girlfriend by the hand and hold her. Doing it in front of your friends, her friends and in public will often gain extra points. Be careful not to do the possessive, "ur my bitch" wrist grab here. That makes you look like an asshole.

A Night on the Town –

Take your girlfriend out to dinner and drinks, just the two of you. If you have taken dance lessons, it would be good to try that out here. Movies, shows, and special events are also good.

A Romantic Getaway –

Plan a little overnight mini-vacation to help her get relieve the stress of her workweek. Leave on a Friday, come back Saturday or Sunday. You will get extra points if you can work in a destination with romantic sights and drinks with umbrellas. Think beaches and waterfalls.

A Passionate Kiss –

Kiss her for no good reason. Make it an eye popping magical fireworks sort of kiss. Then smile at her and give no reason why you did it other than because you absolutely had to taste her kiss at that very moment.

A "No Good Reason" Gift –

If she points out something she likes in a store, go back when she's not looking and grab it. Give it to her for no good reason. Pair this up with a weekend get away or a nice dinner.

Be Her First And Last Compliment –

Everyday, start your day by telling her one thing you love about her.. Then, no matter how the day went, make sure you end the day with something else positive. Compliment her.

Drop the L-bomb –

Once in a while for no reason at all, just look at her and say you love her.

Tell Her Why She's Special –

Tell your girl what it is that makes her perfect. Don't wait for a special moment, just tell her, or send a text, email, etc.

Get Her a Card –

Grab a greeting card on your way home from work. Hide it in her purse or just leave it for her to find.

Include Her –

Just when she thinks you are going to go do something with only the boys. Change course and include her. Take her golfing, shooting, playing pool, to the bar, etc. Let her see how the boy's play. Let your buddies know ahead of time if you plan to crash a regularly scheduled event such as Poker Night with your girl.

Talk Dirty

Once you've been together for a while, send her an absolutely shocking, earth shaking mind bending dirty text message or just call her up and do it. Make it a Penthouse Forum moment. Don't do it too soon or too often though or you look like a stalker freak.

Ham It Up –

Do something completely cheesy such as making a heart out of red rose petals on the bed and lay one single red rose in the middle. Light the room with candles and lead her to it blindfolded. Kiss her neck as you remove the blindfold.

Erotic Gifts

As a general rule, you need to really know somebody before you buy her an erotic gift. It is not your best plan to show up on a first date with a box of condoms, the jumbo tub of lube and the game Twister. Actually in retrospect, it really is no better to take the move Twister with you. I always recommend that you take your girlfriend with you when you buy her an intimate present. Barring this little bit of wisdom, here are some things to consider when you purchase erotic gifts.

1. Unless she has specifically told you that she wants this gift or had a fantasy about this gift, you probably got it for your enjoyment. She knows this.
2. It does not matter if you are the Tantric booty master, you can't compete with the Jumbo Deluxe 63 Horsepower King Kong vibrator. If you are going to get jealous, don't buy it for her.
3. Whether you purchase it for her or not, she may use a vibrator when you are not there. Get over it

and hope she lets you help her with it on occasion.

4. Never have erotic gifts delivered to her workplace.

5. Don't give erotic gifts in front of her family.

6. Not all women like erotic gifts.

7. The dirtier the gift, the better you have to know her to get away with it.

8. Always get two sets of handcuff keys.

9. Sometimes the erotic hot and tingly formula can feel like your junk is on fire.

10. Know what the gift does before you give it to her.

11. Remote control vibrators can be lots of fun unless the neighbor's remote is on the same frequency... then its just wrong. It's even worse if it's their TV remote.

12. "Looks cool" and "feels good" can be mutually exclusive.

13. Never buy "used."

14. If her response to the gift is "Ummmm wow..." You may wanna check out the section on screw ups. Or give her more shots of tequila.

Engaging Propositions

When things are going well enough that you can't imagine being without her, it is time to propose. By this time, you should know your girl well enough that you can probably come up with ideas of your own. However, here are a few things to consider before proposing and some proposal ideas to get you going.

When you consider proposing, the first thing to consider is timing. If she has a lot going on in her life or if you have recently done something colossally stupid, it is a bad time to propose. Hold off until it is right so that the moment is one she will always remember.

Second, know what she likes before you propose. Know what kind of ring, including size, she dreams of. Know what she might consider the perfect proposal so that you can aim for it. Whatever you do, do it honestly here. If you can afford a ¼ carat from WalMart, get that and present it with pride. If you can afford 2 carats from Tiffany's then get that. Don't try to pass one off as the other. A cubic zirconia in a Tiffany's box may seem really smart in your head, but it is really not a great plan. When she goes to have the ring appraised, she will feel stupid and you will get dumped.

The final and probably most important thing to remember when you propose is that the proposal is about her. You are asking a person you love to put everything at stake and agree to be in your life forever. I am a firm believer that you should go big or go home when it comes to your proposal. Get the nicest ring and plan the nicest proposal you can dream up. If it happens, it will be a memory she should have forever. If you are the slightest bit unsure of her answer, you may want to go with a proposal that is more discrete and leaves her with a way to say no and not humiliate you. The higher you fly, the more you risk, but the payout is more fun in the end. Have some idea of what you will do if she says, "no." As a man, you can either get all pissed off and stomp away or you can use the "no" as a way to build a stronger relationship that may later lead to "yes."

Some starter ideas for you to tailor to your individual girl include:

The Classic –

The classic proposal is simple, elegant, and intimate. For this proposal, the man sets up a quiet time and place where he will be nicely dressed and with a ring. The man waits for the perfect moment, looks her in

the eyes and says... "I have something to ask you."
When she says what, he drops to one knee, pulls out the
ring, and fumbles through his great romantic speech.

Pros: Simple and very inexpensive except for the ring.
This also gives the man an opportunity to save face if
she says no.

Cons: It is entirely up to the man, his speech, and his
ring to make this moment perfect.

Surprise, Surprise, Surprise –

Like the classic, this begins with just the man
and the woman at some quiet spot. However, the man
has enlisted the help of a waiter, host or other co-
conspirator to hide the ring in a glass of champagne,
dessert, or other clever little location. As the woman
goes to take a bite, drink, etc. the attentive man will
say... "Hey, what's that in your..." As she discovers the
ring, the man will throw out the proposal.

Pros: A little flashy. Shows some prior planning and a
desire to please. Still leaves some level of ability to save
face if she says, "no."

Cons: If your girl is the flashy type, this may not be quite enough. It is, however, a true classic with nearly universal appeal. If you don't warn the girl and she swallows the ring, the retrieval process could be ugly. Memorable, but ugly.

Two for One –

Buy a pendant or other small jewelry item and have it engraved with the words Marry Me? Take your girl someplace nice and give it to her. While she is reading the back, bring out the ring and propose.

Pros: Two pieces of jewelry. Women like shiny objects and here you are giving away two of them. It can be played as the classic proposal where it is just you and her or you can have the first jewelry item delivered to add a little of the surprise flair. Still leaves room to duck and cover if she says, "No."

Cons: Cost of two pieces of jewelry.

The Cocktail Party –

Invite all of you and your girlfriend's friends and significant people to a big cocktail party. When everyone is getting along well, interrupt the party, make a touching speech, and ask her to marry you. You may want to clue in some of the key people ahead of time such as her parents and your parents to ensure that this goes more smoothly.

Pros: She can show off the ring immediately and has all of the people she would normally call present for the event. It lets her be the absolute center of attention. This can be done as a surprise party or a party she helps plan.

Cons: There is no out if she says no. The ring will get immediate attention from a lot of people. It had better be good.

Guess Who's Here –

When your girlfriend is out of town, preferably with several of her closest friends. Contact someone she will be with and arrange for them to be at a specific place at a specific time. Show up just long enough to propose. For illustrative purposes, here is the ideal scenario:

Your girlfriend is in New York with some friends on a girl's weekend. You buy a ring from Tiffany's. You arrange for one of her friends to go in and ask for something that will alert the staff that it is time to get you. You walk out in a tux with a ring and tell her that you only flew into town to propose. When you have her answer, you let her continue her fun with the girls, fly home and don't interrupt the girls weekend any further

Pros: This one gets extra points for difficulty if you can pull it off. It is complicated and a little Machiavellian, but her friends will certainly see the value in a man like you.

Cons: If she says no, you are broken hearted and broke in a strange city.

Sing a Song –
Take your girl to a karaoke bar and sing her a love song. At the end of the song, hit your knee and

capitalize on an open mike to propose in front of the whole bar.

Pros: Not likely to be forgotten. Probably some free alcohol in it for you and her.

Cons: Nothing like being rejected in a bar full of drunks who think they can sing.

Advertising for Love –

Take out an ad in a paper or magazine you know your girl likes. Say something heartfelt and ask her to read it when it comes out.

Pros: Definitely big depending on the publication. Gives her something she can keep to remember the moment in addition to the ring. Can call her friends and just point out the ad over the phone as she tells them about it.

Cons: Cost is directly proportional to the quality of the ad. A full color ad in a reputable publication is going to be expensive whereas a cheap one liner in the local rag won't cost much. Hard to convince your friends you weren't shot down if the plan fails and you can be sure your nearest and dearest friends will keep a copy around to use as a decoration when you come to visit.

Fun in the Dark –

Pay the local theater to run a proposal in the before movie advertising. Take her there and watch the look on her face when she sees the ad. Propose in the dark.

Pros: Big and flashy way to go. Looks good and is generally pretty cost effective. More anonymous than other big ideas without sacrificing the "wow factor."

Cons: Knee sticks to floor when you kneel down to propose. Any other couples in the room with the same names as you and your girl get in a big fight and it's hard to hear the movie.

Holiday Proposal –

Make Christmas something to remember. Wrap a number of small, inexpensive gifts and put them under the tree for her. After she has opened them and tried so hard not to be disappointed by your total lack of investment in the holiday process, you say you have one more little gift. Pull out the ring and kneel down under the mistletoe. If she likes big family Christmas parties, you could couple this with the Cocktail party idea above to make it a little flashier.

Pros: Can be a private and quiet way to go or it can be as big as you want. Definitely gets you off the hook for the crappy presents before it.

Cons: Competing with Christmas may or may not be successful.

Spur of the Moment –

Take her to Vegas and ask her to go to one of the chapels and look around. While you are there, propose and see if she will do it on the spot. If the Gods are smiling and you've been drinking at the blackjack table all day long, you just might have a wife before it's over.

Pros: Only you and she know what happened in Vegas.

Cons: Violates most of a woman's ideas about a perfect wedding or proposal. You both may wake up hung over and freaked out.

Stop in the Name of the Law –
If you've got the connections, arrange a ride along with the local police and have her pulled over. When she is stopped use the loud speaker to remove her from the car and have her face away from you. With the light on her so that she can't see who is coming up. Approach and kneel. Have the officer tell her to turn around and kill the light. When her eyes adjust, she will see you kneeling there with a big ring in hand. Pop the question.

Pros: It is memorable and will be caught on a dashcam.

Cons: She had better have a killer sense of humor and the ring better make up for the stress you just caused.

A Bigger Buy One, Get One Deal
Take her out and shop for a car that will be "her" car. After she picks it and the papers are signed. Have the salesman hide the ring in the center console or glove box. When you get in the car, insist on driving, and ask

her to get something from the hiding place for you. While she is searching, pull over. When she finds it, propose.

Pros: Big and memorable.

Cons: Dude… you just bought a car for her.

Tip: Wanna impress that Gold Digger in your life? Do this one with a house.

Biggest Game in Town –

If you have the money or connections, you can always turn a major league sporting event into your own personal wedding forum. The easy out is to use the big board to flash the proposal. If you have the biggest brass balls in town and a checkbook to match, you might even be able to get out on the field of play during halftime to hit your knee in front of a crowd of 75000 screaming football fans.

Pros: Nobody has done it much bigger.

Cons: If you fail, you fail on national TV and later on You-tube and again on a blooper special and possibly on videotape at your friend's house at every football party for the next five years.

Tip: Kneeling down on the 50 yard line at an NFL game is big. Doing it at the local high school game is just not so cool unless one of you is the coach or a teacher.

That Was Dumb

Sooner or later you are going to screw things up somehow. Depending on what you did and how you did it, there may be ways that you can save your relationship if you are so inclined. With all good screw-ups, there are several steps that you need to go through before you can even begin to talk to the woman in your life about your malfunction.

First, you need to sit down and decide if you want to save your relationship. A critical introspective look at your life is needed here. If you are only with your girl out of a sense of comfort or security and there is really no love left, your screw up may have been a subconscious or conscious attempt to sabotage your relationship so that you could get out. If this is the case, it would be best to be honest with yourself and your girl at this point because your recovery plan may be much more complicated than you are willing and able to do.

Second, you need to be prepared to be fully honest and answer any uncomfortable questions that may be thrown at you by your girlfriend. In the case of big, big screw-ups, you may want to lie to protect her, but this won't help you. If a woman is really in tune with you, she already knows the story before you try to tell it. Lying here, even if it is for the right reasons, is gonna make the whole problem worse.

She gonna be mad. The level of mad has a direct correlation to the size of your screw up and your level of honesty and willingness to make things right. If your behavior was merely inconsiderate, the level of mad may only last a little while. If your actions shook her whole perception of you, she gonna be mad for a long time.

How to Start

The first step in determining what to do is to look at what you've done. If you failed to read the chapter on practical jokes or you did something that was really pretty small, you do not need to act like it was the crime of the century. However, if your screw up involves her trust, her money, her safety, or her future; you better be ready to put a solid plan in place to save your relationship.

No matter what happened, it is better if she hears it from you than on the streets. The old adage deny til you die could literally result in your death here. The problem is only getting worse if she hears about your screw-up and you have missed several good opportunities to come clean before she found out.

Small Screw Ups

When you just piss her off because you are rude, insensitive, or think you are funny when you are not. You can handle it pretty quick with a sincere apology. I recommend using this format.

"I'm sorry I, _____. Looking back I realize that I should have _____."

If this works, you probably guessed right and the problem is not too huge. If she wants to discuss it or verbally beat your ass for it a little bit, let her. Your goal here is to let the problem resolve and be done as quickly as possible. Expect a 2-8 hour turn around on fixing this fuck up.

Medium or Ongoing Screw-ups

These screw-ups can range from one big event or an ongoing trend that affects the way she sees herself or the relationship. If you are consistently cold or distant or if you have a onetime event where you tell her to "leave me the fuck alone," you are in medium screw-up land.

Other events in this category would be taking off with your <u>male</u> buddies and ending up on a two day bender where you "forget" to call, shaving her favorite pet or converting the garage where she parks her car to your man cave without telling her.

A screw up of this size is going to take a little more massaging before you are safely out of the woods and back in happy relationship land. Expect at least a week to fix this one.

With a medium screw up, you need to survive the initial storm. Then you need to work on fixing the problem. To weather the storm, I would suggest finding a nice out of the way restaurant or bar where you can go and have your ass publicly beat. Find a place where you can have some privacy but still have it be neutral territory. I recommend having one place for the ass beatings because the visits to this restaurant are going to cause you some post traumatic stress if your girl does her job right. Normally the public venue provides enough distractions to prevent you from acting like an asshole when she gets mad. This works in your favor. If there was any doubt, you are buying dinner, appetizer, drinks, and dessert.

When she is beating your ass, listen to her. You have no idea how to fix the problem if you are not clear on what part made her mad. If you are truly unsure as to why she is mad, ask her what part of your behavior made her the angriest. When you understand, tell her you understand. If you've been listening here, you will have some idea of how to fix your screw-up.

Now it gets a little dicey. You need to fix your screw up without being insincere. Women can detect insincere like sharks can detect blood in the water. You are better off apologizing and shutting your mouth of you can't sincerely try to find a solution. If you are willing and able to find a solution, I would suggest some language like this:

"I'm sorry I, _____. Looking back I realize that I should have

_____. You are important to me and I would like to try to make things better. Would it help if I _____."

If you got it right, she will probably beat your ass with some comments about how you wouldn't have really done it if you thought she was that important, but she will either buy off on your plan or she will suggest other things to help. If you didn't get it right, you are going to go another lap down the ass-beating trail. Eventually, she will either tire and let you off the hook or she will give you ideas on how to fix it.

The Biggie

When one of these happens, the man has either had a string of medium screw-ups or has have done something so big that it makes your girl completely re-evaluate who you are and what your relationship is. When it is inspired by a single event, it is normally an event of such huge proportions that the man's first thought is "Oh shit... if she finds out... how do I hide this." Mistakes of this size normally involve trust and fidelity.

A screw up of this size is not one that will be presented to her in public, but you can count on the negotiations on how to fix it being held at your favorite "ass beating" restaurant. As a man, you should tell your woman of your screw up on her turf and with as much tact as you possess. Don't lie. When you begin to wonder if public discussion time is really a good plan, remember that the point of the public negotiation is to make the man behave. If your relationship survives The Biggie, then it is truly worth being in because a screw up of this size is normally a deal breaker and the man will need to do some serious work to get things back on track. The minimum recovery on this is a month, but the man can expect that it will come back as a reminder for a good long time.

When a man makes this happen, he needs to be prepared for tears, anger, possibly the silent treatment, and maybe even a complete moratorium on contact for a while. The man will need to use this time to really decide what he wants his relationship to be with this woman. If he wants the relationship, he needs to keep going back and being in her life as much as he can until she either tells him its over for good and to go away or she opens communication lines again. During this time period, the man should not start dating or finding new women unless he has made a formal break from his current girlfriend. The last thing a man should want here is to have his current girlfriend thinking about getting back together and catching him in public or private with another woman.

Once the initial period of anger and fighting is over, the process gets remarkably similar to that of the medium screw up. The number of ass beatings and the amount of reconciliation that the man should be prepared for, however, is much higher. If you chose your favorite sports bar for your ass beating location, you will know you have a big screw up happening if you are hoping that the T.V. mount above you will just break so the T.V. can fall on your head and kill you.

Now is the time when the man must decide if he is truly in or out with this girl. She has opened the door and the man should know that the cost would be high. If she is worth it to him, he should take the chance. If he has any doubts at all, now is the time to walk away.

A word of caution… her friends know. They knew before you got home from your first talk. They hate you right now. They will help her hide your body and are advising her to get out before she really gets hurt. Understand that this is a good thing. They are protecting her. Don't bash them or get too worked up, this is The Sisterhood at work. You don't have to just earn back your girl's trust; you have to earn back her friends' trust.

A word of caution part deux… When you tell your friends, they will have "helpful advice" and plans to ensure that you are okay. Before you take their grand advice, you probably need to know that "okay" to your friends means that you are back in the pack as one of the boys. When you receive advice from your friends, I would suggest you carefully evaluate their advice to determine if it is likely to help or hurt the situation. Most of the time, you would be better off ignoring their help especially if it involves tequila and cell phones, Guinness and Strippers, or any plan involving your ex-girlfriend.

Great Man Thinking That Doesn't Work
For screw-ups of every size, men have certain thought processes. Some key ones to discredit are listed here.

She Won't Catch Me
Yes she will. The Sisterhood has already caught you and they just haven't figured out what to do with you yet or who to report it to. If you have somehow avoided all of the obvious pitfalls of your actions, your girl still has "that feeling." She may not know exactly what you did, but she knows you did some bullshit. She's also consulting The Sisterhood on how to catch you.

My Plan Can't Fail

Do you remember Wile E. Coyote and the Roadrunner? The man is the Coyote in this scenario. The man is absolutely certain that he is a supergenius. Unbeknownst to him the woman has already stepped over the trap, eaten the food, and put the dynamite in his shorts. The minute a man thinks he can't get caught, he will.

I'm Protecting Her by Lying

This is an easy one for men to justify because it fits nicely into the social stereotype of women being the weaker sex that needs protecting from men and because it allows men to rationalize deceptive behavior. Despite their lifelong training, men need to realize that it this really doesn't work because you will be compounding a screw-up with a lie. When you do this, you get an almost immediate upward shift in severity. Your small just got ugly and your medium now threatens your relationship.

Attempting to further use this one by coupling it with the fact that it occurred before you were together or while you were broken up does not help. If you have things in your past that you just don't want her to know, you should say that you don't want to talk about it. This might be a tough conversation, but it is about half as tough as getting caught lying.

A Gift Will Fix It

No… No, it won't. When a man really screws up, the only women that will really be okay after a gift purchase is the Gold Diggers. All of the other women will look at the gift and think…

> *Fantastic, I have received some good old fashioned "Sorry I fucked the hoochie at the bar" diamonds.*

The Golddigger with think…

> *Nice diamonds, I should introduce him to my hoochie friends so I can get some more.*

The last thing you want to do is associate the gift giving process with your screw-ups. Save gifts for when things are good. A token of love during the big fight may shut her up for a few minutes, but you can believe that the fight ain't over.

Screaming and Avoidance Will Help

Yeah, this one will help. It will help your woman decide you need to be gone from her life. When you are wrong, take your lumps and fix the problem. Don't have a screaming, kicking, crybaby tantrum because you got caught and are now being held accountable.

Once you get over the urge to scream, it is also important to recognize that the silent treatment is gonna end equally as bad. If you are in the throws of a well-deserved ass beating on the phone, it is normally best to let it run its course. Announcing, "we are not talking about this," and hanging up is only going to make things worse. If she calls you back, the ass beating starts over and includes your most recent good plan of slamming the phone down. If she doesn't call you back, it may be wise to hire a team of seasoned and veteran bodyguards because without them you gonna die.

I Got This
When you screw up, you are no longer in control. Before you are caught, you are at risk of being exposed by everyone who knows about your screw up. When you get caught, you are actually not the victim here, she is and she ain't gonna let you forget it. After you are caught, you have a responsibility to repair the damage you've done.

The screw up was the only part of this process that you controlled and you apparently didn't do that very well. Everything after that was just leading you down the inevitable trail of getting caught and fixing your malfunction.

She Probably Won't Even Care

Are you high? Of course she will care. If you have to think this thought, you have probably already screwed up or you are about to screw up in a way that could get your picture posted on the back of a milk carton. Occasionally, they may act like they don't care but to be perfectly honest, I have found that women often care the most about the things we don't understand. Whatever you are doing should probably stop if you have this thought. If you have already done it, I would go ahead and confess now.

I Don't Need Help

Maybe you really do. Maybe you haven't just coincidentally found yourself with 74 consecutive crazy women. Maybe you make them that way. If your fights always have the same theme and you can't seem to control it (i.e. impulse control, drinking, drug use, gambling, or violence) then you need to take a look at your life and make some hard decisions. It never hurt anyone to get a professional evaluation to determine if they have things that could be solved through lifestyle changes and/or counseling. If your relationship is worth it, you will do it. If it is not, you need to realize that changing girls won't change the problem.

Conclusion

Here is a handy little reference to help you make those critical man decisions

DO	*DON'T*
Call her	Call her 94 times at work
Kiss her cheek	Lick her cheek
Play with her	Play games with her
Tell her jokes	Make her the butt of jokes
Watch her sleep	Watch her sleep through binoculars
Pull her chair out	Pull her chair out from under her
Buy her a drink	Put roofies in her drink
Get a little jealous	Get violently jealous
Get a little kinky	Chain her in a basement dungeon
Talk dirty	Talk dirty to her best friend
Take her to a movie	Post porno movies of her on the internet
Tell her you love her	Burn a heart into her lawn

Try to reconcile	Stalk her
Fight passionately	Hurt her
Have friends	Exclude her from your friends
Put her first	Forget that she deserves to be first
Take charge	Boss her around
Let her take charge	Give up
Give	Take
Take	Give
Fix the hurts	Cause new hurts
Chase her	Chase her in your car down a lonely road
Let her keep some clothes at your house	Wear her clothes
Give her a beautiful ring	Ask for the ring back – it was a gift dumbass
Buy her gifts	Buy her gifts because you screwed up
Take her breath away	Take her breath away by holding a pillow over her face
Grab a breath mint	Skip brushing
Hold her	Hold her hostage

Essentially, the point of this book is to say that relationships take two people to work properly. The man and the woman need to be equals because in a relationship where there is a disparity in power, nobody is fulfilled. Relationships are hard. To succeed in a fast paced world, a couple has to constantly chase one another. Be kind, gentle, and attentive. Help her when she wants it and support her with a bemused smile the rest and life will go swimmingly.

Not every relationship will make it and this book just presents half of the story. If the man is doing all he can to make it right and the relationship fails anyway, it was probably doomed from the start. A man who tries is a rare creature indeed. If word of your behavior gets out to your friends, it may get you some grief. If word of your behavior gets out to The Sisterhood, it may get you a fantastic woman who is willing to take one more chance at finding Mr. Right.

Once the sisterhood drops that perfect woman in your lap, try not to screw it up. Not all women are the same so you can't assume that whatever you did with your crazy ex-girlfriend will work with the new and saner girlfriend you have now. To keep harmony at home try to help out more and exercise your ego less. If you don't know where to go next don't just thrash around and guess. Women are natural communicators so when you are in doubt about where your relationship is heading, what gift to give, her interests, her pet peeves, or just her life in general; ask her. You will be glad you did.